Patrick Conghey

Poems Dusted Off

By
Patrick Confrey

Old Poems
(extended version)

ISBN: 978-1-910179-01-7

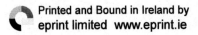

Printed and Bound in Ireland by
eprint limited www.eprint.ie

This collection of poetry is dedicated to the memory of John B. Hanney, who died suddenly on 10th February the 1991 late of the central sorting office in Sheriff Street.

You left us without a goodbye,
And left your friends.
High and dry.
Your kindnesses were small,
But they were many.
I remember you for that John Hanney.
You were indeed a true friend,
I liked your company until the end,
And sometimes the money you lent.
Goodbye for the work breaks
We spent.

RIP.

Table of Contents

Acknowledgements

This collection of poetry is a continuation of my earlier collection called ' Poems Dusted off '. But there are new poems here starting with the poem Agony Aunt, and from then on. Some of these poems deal with the sadness of emigration, and the economic collapse in Ireland. There are a few poems of faith here also, and a poem in memory of Seamus Heaney. I hope these new poems are of interest. The passing of Seamus Heaney in August 2013 was a loss to the world of literature. Seamus was unique in that he had no envy towards other writers, and poets, and he always acknowledged good literature wherever he saw it. Seamus Heaney was dedicated to literature. He cannot be replaced RIP. I wish to thank all the staff at eprint Blanchardstown for help in bringing out this collection of poetry, and thanks to all others who helped out.

Patrick Confrey
2014

PART ONE

Introduction

The poems in part one, of this collection, cover various issues such as the environment, the troubles in Beirut and the Lebanon, during the 1980,s, and moral and social issues. The poems on Beirut I call the Beirut poems. One poem in the collection condemns the exploitation of immigrants during the so-called Celtic Tiger years. There is also some satire in Part I.

Part two mainly consists of nature poems. I wrote these poems in Edmondstown near Rockbrook, during the 1980,s, when I lived there. At that time it was country, with unspoiled fields, and hedgerows, and so it was possible to write these poems, but I could not write them now. Most of these poems were written during the 1980's, with some exceptions. Rockbrook, and Tibradden, are mentioned in a few poems. The Owendoher River, which is mentioned, flows through Edmondstown, Ballyboden, and Willbrook, and it flows into the Dodder River, at Bushy Park. Allen's pub, which is mentioned, became known as Doherty's, or Rock Taverns, for a time. It is now known as THE MERRY PLOUGHBOY pub, and it is known for traditional music, and dancing.

NO FAME

No fame is mine,
Nor shall in time,
No sneak previews,
No interviews,
No mention,
On the news.
Just simple poems in a
Copybook, written and
Forsook,
I will just be myself,
A dusty poet,
On the shelf.

NEVER SHOOK

I wrote poems, that never shook,
Forsaken in copy books,
Like the murmur of a sleepy brook,
People went by,
No heed they took.

I wrote them for what
They're worth,
Like a new born child at birth.

Maybe a girl,
Maybe a boy,
Maybe the cause of joy.

Is there any point in this pursuit,
Much like wearing a too old suit,
I may give it up to tell the truth

During the early 1980's Beirut, and the Lebanon were a battleground between rival militias, culminating in suicide lorry bomb blasts, which brought the world to the brink of war. These Beirut poems were written during that unhappy period.

OH BEIRUT

Oh Beirut, Beirut,
Your name is hell,
With gunfire,
And rocket shell.
And people blown up,
Their only crime,
In the wrong place,
At the wrong time.
And hatred, and actions brute,
Beirut, Beirut.

BEIRUT BLASTS

Beirut, Beirut, they bomb, and shoot,
Will there ever be a truce?
Beirut, Beirut,
Another blast,
Even worse than our own
     Belfast.
     Beirut, Beirut,
     The dye is cast,
     Is all hope now gone past?

IN BEIRUT - (1983)

It is now the eleventh hour,
And the nations, with the
Greatest power,
Their weapons, pointed in directions
Four.
Annihilation threat,
While men with no fear of death,
Show greater courage,
But brutality yet.
Devastation unsurpassed,
And vicious lorry bomb blasts,
Suicide bombs, in Beirut,
To tell the truth.
Tearing a country, and a people apart,
Before they made a start.
The thin edge of the wedge,
To push the world over the edge.
Fear of what will happen next,
And Regan vexed.
Worry about loss of oil,
Economies spoil,
Afraid to choose,
Whichever way lose.
While Russia remains aloof,
And foolproof.
I hope that there will be restraint,
Or no one will be left to paint.
Or say who won, all will be gone.

SENTIMENTAL SOD

I am just a sentimental sod,
And I look backwards,
As I forward plod.

I sit and with my thoughts,
Play host,
Boil my tea,
Burn my toast.

Conservation Poems

❧

SPOIL

If we spoil the land,
And don't conserve,
We will get an environment,
That will unnerve.
They're building another road,
Maybe it's only my patience
Goad.
On the motor car's behalf,
The Golden Calf.
Though I once had a car myself,
I didn't think it was God himself.
And some day we might lament,
That we spread around so much
Cement.
But too late then to repent

PRESERVED

Preserved be the trees, and their endow,
Preserved be the fields, where stands the cow,
Preserved be them here and now.

Preserved be the golden cobs of corn,
Preserved be the cherry blossom's adorn,
Preserved be every sunny morn'.

Preserved be the mountain streams, and lakes,
If not for ourselves, for the future's sake.

Preserved be the mountain lands unspoiled,
Preserved be the fruit that's growing wild,
Preserved be the coastline, from being oiled.

Preserved be the seas, where sails the ferry,
Preserved be the briar that holds the berry,
Preserved be every Christmas merry.

PRAYER OF THE UNBORN CHILD

Leave us the seas, and leave them clean,
Leave us the forests, to be seen.
Leave us the summer morning fog,
Don't let our cities, be shrouded in
Smog.
Leave us food, that we can taste,
Kindly dispose of your nuclear waste.
Don't spray our crops with pesticide,
Let us by clean waters reside.
Leave us the bees, to make the honey,
Let us enjoy a day that is sunny.
Leave us Sunday, as a day of rest,
And Mother Nature not molest.

A BRIAR

No way am I a flower,
More I am a briar,
And my poetry of late,
Has gone more to satire.
And it would upset no one,
If I did expire,
Or into monastic life,
I would quietly
Aspire.
And it's vinegar now,
Whenever I perspire.
No, I am no longer sweet,
I'm not what I was prior,
I am gone bitter now,
More I am a briar.

TOOTSIE

I went to see Tootsie,
With my wife,
Dustin Hoffman's performance,
Of life.
While others found it a comedy,
I found it a tragedy.
What about the murder towards
The end,
When Tootsie's life was brought
To an end?
Though funny, I couldn't help
Taking it seriously.
Hoffman painted as a clown,
Two people rolled into one,
But as Tootsie was more fun.
And imagine the audience's rage,
If a clown undressed on stage.
It's as if a personality is
Killed,
And behind the curtains did.
A film that was a comedy,
Rolled into a tragedy.

A DRIED UP LEMON

(A TORMENTOR)
He turns up like a bad penny,
Asking if I have poems any.
I've done the best I could,
But he wants more, he wants blood.
Who does he think I am,
For heaven's sake,
William Blake.
I told him what I think,
I'd recommend to him a shrink.
I've called his attention to Eason's
Store,
With books on poetry galore.
There are books by Durcan, Boland,
And Matthew Sweeney,
And it is all blocked up,
With books by Heaney.
But it's no use,
To give up he did refuse.
I'm a dried up lemon with no juice,
I'll go away till,
My thoughts run loose.

THE SALVATION ARMY LADY SWEET[1]

The Salvation Army lady sweet,
Around the pub, she makes her beat.
People don't think of God or sin,
But they put money in her tin,
As she went by,
Handing out her 'WAR CRY.'
To a man at the bar, she said
'GOD BLESS '.
He stared indifferently into his glass.
He didn't respond,
Or turn his head,
To what she said.
As she left, it struck my mind,
She didn't react,
Though he was unkind.

---

[1] This is a true story. The Salvation Army lady in this poem, used to go around Dublin city centre pubs, in the 1970's, handing out the Salvation Army paper "WAR CRY". She would have a tin with her, in case a customer wanted to give a donation.

POLLUTION AND FOG

The year 2075 A.D. November the 16th.

RTE. 1, 10:00 p.m., television news, and the
Newsreader is Raymond Cusack. It is
10:25 p.m., when the report comes in:
Raymond Cusack, ' Reports are coming in
Of a pile-up on the Stillorgan road,
It isn't known yet how many cars
Are involved, there are no further
Details.'

The weatherman shrugs, we have been
Polluting the atmosphere now for years,
This fog only confirms,
His worst fears.

'No busses,
Are running,
No taxis are coming,
There are no ambulances, to carry the ill,
Very few are working, visibility is nil.
And the Naas Dual Carriageway is blocked,
With abandoned cars,
Lorries, and trucks.
Reports from the Northside, are just the same,
And Dublin Airport, has diverted the planes.
The flights all over have come to a halt,
A dense pall of fog, all over the fault.

An EERIE silence hangs over the docks,
And people stay behind doors,
That are locked.
There's a ship in the harbour unable
To dock,
And the Captain has taken stock,
Calms his passengers,
Reads his book.
An EERIE sound through the fog,
A barking city centre dog.
An army helicopter with night lights,
And infra-red,
Hovers over a city, silent and dead.
While a group of anarchists,
Behind closed doors,
Are hoping the fog, lasts four days more.
'Some said it was Armageddon,
    Some said it was the Second Coming,
    Some said it was environmental
    Disaster.
    Some said the world was in it's last
    Year. '
RTE 1. 10:00 p.m., television news, the next day
November the 17th, It is Raymond Cusack
Reading.
Raymond; ' The dense fog which had
Enshrouded Dublin, and County, for the past
Twenty four hours, has finally
Started to lift, and since 5:00 p.m., this evening
The City, and County, has been returning to
Normal. Here is our outdoor reporter Caroline
Byrne.

Caroline Byrne: 'I am standing here at the
Spawell
Roundabout, near Templeogue, and the scene is
Typical of the whole city, two Gardai are
Examining an abandoned car. Gardai are
working
Flat out in Dublin city, and county, to clear the
Roads of abandoned cars, lorries, and vans. The
Fear is that abandoned vehicles, could become an
Easy target for roaming gangs, taking advantage
of
The almost total breakdown in mobility, caused
by
The worst fog, ever experienced. Amid
Speculation that the fog was caused by years of
Pollution, and urban expansion, we contacted the
Weather Centre, but a spokesman there refused
to Comment. '
This is Caroline Byrne for RTE I, television
news,
At the Spawell roundabout, near Templeogue.

THE END.

CHRISTMAS EVE – A CHRISTMAS POEM

The tiny tots, are in their cots,
And at the end they hang their socks.
Making sure they won't be forgot,
A little to them means a lot.

And soon they fall asleep,
And round the door,
Their mother peeps,
Then back down the stairs she creeps.

Little boy is hoping the snow will fall,
Little girl is waiting on her doll,
Decorations hang on the wall.

There are Christmas tree lights, and
Presents that weigh,
And neighbours calling in to say:
'A happy Christmas to all within '
And raise a glass of sherry or gin,

Christmas cards on the mantelpiece,
And all around an air of peace.

DICKENS'S GHOSTS[2]

I saw Dickens's ghosts,
Of past, present,
And to come.
Christmas past was smiling,
    Christmas present none.
    In one hand he had a rifle,
    In another hand a bomb.
    Christmas future would not show,
    What it held,
    He did not know.

---

[2] This poem may seem obscure, but the ghost of Christmas past was smiling because he had lived through a time of peace. Christmas present has a rifle in one hand, and a bomb in the other, because he was living through a time of violence. The ghost of Christmas future would not show, because he did not know the future.

MY ISLAMIC FRIEND MARTHA[3]

We met on the gardening course,
And we did discourse.
Me a Christian to this date,
She was rock solid,
In her Islamic faith.
We got to know her brief,
Unshakable in her belief.
Yet dressed as a modern woman,
As she can,
While living by her Koran.

We built a bridge of tolerance,
And learned not to take offence,
From what was done,
And what was said,
As we tended to the vegetable
Beds.
But now the course is at an end,
I have lost my Islamic friend.
No more will we turn the sod,
But maybe with the help,
Of God,
For all the loss,
Someday again,
Our paths, may cross.

---

[3] This is a true story written in 2009, coming near the end of the gardening course at Airfield Trust, Kilmacud, Dublin. Martha is married and she lives in Ballinteer, in Dublin.

IF

(ABOUT MYSELF)
If God could see inside,
My soul,
How I extol,
What I desire,
What I aspire.

I wish that I could retreat,
To what I was,
When I was sweet.

When I was pure,
Before I found
Literature.

Then I could
Look beyond vanity,
To a bigger picture,
A greater humanity.

I see my writings,
What I have put out,
And all I want,
Is an exit out.

GOOD RIDDANCE CELTIC TIGER

Good riddance Celtic tiger beast,
Only a few, came to your feast.
The thousands of immigrants who
Came to our shore,
Through the revolving door,
Gone home once more.

The immigrants, who graced the
Stage,
And worked in Ireland, for a low wage,
Now just a statistic on the page.

Like the Celtic tiger,
They are gone like the mist.,
Their names forgotten,
And not missed.
Like an old commodity,
On a shopping list.

IMMIGRANTS

They are not an invasion,
But a new equation,
Going forward,
A new nation.

Going forward,
We can embrace,
A different culture,
A different face,
In a new place.

Going forward,
New plans,
Different clans,
In a new land.

RACIAL BARRIER BROKEN

I observed it in the newsagent shop,
Called' BUS STOP.'
The Dublin woman shop assistant,
In an instant.
She saw the Chinese woman,
She hadn't seen for a while,
They hugged each other,
And a smile.
The racial barrier broken,
In a single act,
Nothing spoken.
And it all happened,
In an instant,
Between the two shop
Assistants.

HUMIDITY - AN AUGUST THUNDERSTORM

It was not the temperature,
But the humidity high,
The answer to the question why,
The thunderstorm, came at morning,
Came as it were without warning.
After two days of sweated brow,
No sign of it did show.
The warmth that turned to haze,
And moisture dims, the distant gaze.
Late August thunderstorm,
From the southeast, it came from.
The sky darkened there first,
Before over the city burst.
It was gone again within the hour,
But showed its momentary power.
The lightening that did no harm,
But showed the power of thunderstorm.

SOCIAL INJUSTICE[4]

Social injustice now is rife[5],
The worker's hours are cut,
With a knife,
And what happened to the job,
For life.
From Dublin to London,
And back up to Fife,
Prepare ourselves,
For industrial strife.

---

[4] Written in 2009.
[5] Rife, meaning widespread.

PETTY JEALOUSY

I've seen a lot of grab, and greed,[6]
And I've turned my back,
And paid no heed.
And when unkind words were said,
I just let on I never heard.
But there's one fault I can't
Harbour,
Petty jealousy, I abhor.
And it's rampant, throughout the
Land.
And along with greed walks hand,
In hand.
And what's more I'll bet my socks,
It was never confessed,
In a confession box.

---

[6] Thou shalt not covet thy Neighbours poetry!

NOT MUCH SOUGHT - A SATIRE

My poetry is not much sought,
Would anyone mind, if I was,
An astronaut.
Trying to get home on a COSMIC RAY.
They would rather out in space I'd stay.

Would they send out a space shuttle,
No they would rather,
I would scuttle.
Maybe end up on the planet Mars.
They'd be happy then I'd be far.

Yes on some distant planet marooned,
The radio broken,
And not tuned.
And they wouldn't bother trying to
Trace her,
Some have said, I am a spacer.
And the world would be happier,
If this did,
Of me and my poetry,
It would be rid..

THE SARDINE TIN

The situation I didn't sus,
Saturday evening,
And the 15b bus.
And it being Saturday evening,
The shoppers,
They were teeming.
And it pulls in,
The sardine tin.
Then there's no queue,
And civility gone,
In desperation, to get on.
And why the determination,
Isn't it daft,
One would think, we were
Boarding a life raft.
A fear of been left behind,
Another bus to find,
A fear it would miss you,
A life or death issue.

USING WORDS

A poet can use words like magic,
Paint a picture,
Happy or tragic.
Stand the words,
Upon their head,
When they are tired,
Tuck them into bed.
Glue them together,
Like jelly set,
Hang them on the clothesline,
When they get wet.
Juggle them over his head,
In the morning give them jam,
On their bread.

TOO LATE

Too late now for ambition,
I've given my last rendition.
To late now wealth to seek,
I'd be better my sense of
Values to keep.
Too late now to make new friends,
I'd be better old bridges to mend.
Too late for me to go sweet,
Into myself,
I'll probably retreat.
Too late to visit far off places,
I'm too lazy to pack big cases.
Too late for me to make a start,
I haven't got the heart.
      Too late to take a challenge on,
I'll content myself,
      With poetry, and song

END OF PART ONE.

PART TWO

⌘

Introduction

The poems in part two are mainly nature poems. The Owendoher River, which is mentioned, flows down through Rockbrook, and then through Edmondstown, Ballyboden, and Willbrook. It then flows through Rathfarnham Village, and it flows into the Dodder River, at Bushy Park. Allen's pub, which is mentioned, is just down from Rockbrook. It has changed hands several times. For a while it was known as Doherty's, or Rock Taverns. It is now known as the 'Merry Ploughboy pub. These poems were written in the early 1980's, when the area was virgin fields, and hedgerows. In more recent times houses, and apartments have been built in Edmondstown. The Merry Ploughboy pub is now well known for traditional Irish music, and dancing.

WALK TO ROCKBROOK

And the road to Rockbrook,
I took,
Where flows the Owendoher,
And while the time, watching out
For wild flowers.
And I saw iris yellow,[7]
Where shades the beech, oak,
And willow.
And sleepy mallard ducks, that
Swim upstream,
And young trout that break the brim.
Hawthorn grows a plenty too,
Stop off at Allen's pub, to admire
The view.
Then down to Tibradden go,
Where rockrose grows in hedgerow.
Eventually back to housing estates,
Before too late.
Satisfy me,
To be home for tea.

---

[7] Iris Yellow is a beautiful, reed like plant, which grows wildly along riverbanks, and beside ponds. Tibradden, and Rockbrook, are in the foothills of the Dublin Mountains. Allen's pub is now known as the Merry Ploughboy pub.

WALK NEAR PINE FOREST

The road near Pine Forest walk,
On a winter's evening,
Going towards dark.
And only a slight wind to chill,
And up ahead,
The peaceful hills.
The rooks roost,
And from the trees called,
The trees bald.
The trees that silhouette,
Against a yellow sunset.
A sky that's mostly clear,
And a coolness,
In the air.

THROUGH THE SEASONS

WINTER POEMS

‫❧

MID JANUARY SNOW

Better the snow came when it
Should,
Than come in March,
And do no good.
Better the snow did impale,
On road, on roof, on car,
On rail.
And muffled children,
Did avail.
It threw it's blanket dead,
During night's sleepy bed.
It froze, and tried to drift,
And in the wind, did shift.
Remembering back to last spring,
When growing there was
Nothing.
When the milder weather,
Should be here,
Sleet, and hail showers
Appeared.
But now that snow,
It's vengeance vent,
Maybe in spring,
It will relent.

JANUARY SUNRISE

The late sunrise,
Over fields frozen,
Supposing.
The snow in a thin layer,
And a freezing air.
And of clouds, there are
None,
And the temperature,
Minus one.

> And I saw grey heron on heavy wing,
> And wondered how things were
> With him.
> So much of the food, on which he
> Relied,
> Now gone to shelter,
> Gone to hide.
> A sunrise that would not entice,
> A sun that rose,
> Over snow and ice.

WINTER FORECAST

Better now the snow and frost,
Than later on to pay the cost.
They're saying it will be a
Winter mild,
But how can they make such
Predictions wild?
They may be right,
More or less,
But why bother with the guess?
Suffice it to state,
The colder winters,
Often start late.

THE THAW

After the freeze, came the thaw.
And foraging in the fields,
The rook, and Jackdaw.
A temporary ease,
The birds are pleased.
A chance to feed and store,
A winter that's old,
But far from over.

THE MALE CHAFFINCHES[8]

The male chaffinches, that did invade,
With us through the winter stayed.
And they fed along the river,
And in the thicket.
And now and then, the garden visit.
A bit of colour they would flash,
That now and then, the eye would
Catch.

---

[8] During the winter months, Chaffinches often flock together, and feed in parks, hedgerows, and gardens, sometimes with other finches.

WINTER'S SLEEP - A FEBRUARY POEM

They're saying,
It's all over spoken,
That winter's back is broken.
That it brought only a token.
Maybe it's sleeping,
Not awoken.

Don't deride the winter,
Quite this soon,
With the sun still low in the sky,
At noon.
From the middle of January,
To the middle of Feb',
You won't see spiders,
Out building their webs.

So stockpile the logs,
And stockpile the food,
We're out of the trees,
Not out of the wood.

THROUGH THE SEASONS

SPRING POEMS

∞

EARLY CHORUS

The birds in early morning chorus,
Knowing spring is now before us.
After a winter long that wore us.

But I hope the birds,
Are not upset,
By cold spells,
That might come yet,
Because the weather right now,
Is pet.

And the trees are showing,
Signs of caution,
Of growth,
They have no notion.
They are showing such good sense,
A winter that's old,
But not past tense.

THROUGH THE SEASONS

SUMMER POEMS

❧

MAY WEATHER 1984

After the heat wave, came the chill,
And cooler days,
With clouds they fill,
And old and wizened daffodils.
But there is no need,
For remorse,
We still have the flaming gorse.
Other flowers are slow to bloom,
We'll see them at their best,
In June.
A summer that is slow to show
So far,
But still worth,
The waiting for.

MID MAY WEATHER 1984

Mid May and the dry spell broke,
And for hours,
The rain it soaked.
      But it was needed not abhorrent,
      The rain that fell in torrents.
      And for a while pushed away the
      Heat,
      Like a king,
      That lost his seat
      As it were, from his throne,
      It had its time,
      And now is gone.

EARLY AUGUST WEATHER 1984

Now it is early august,
And the weather cooler just.
The July heat incessant,
It has eased,
It has lessened.

For all that heat I would not
Grieve,
Wonder that it left us
Leaves.
Goodbye to all that heat
Incessant,
We can still live,
It is pleasant.
The needed rain, put back life,
What's left of summer?
Now is brief.

THE OWENDOHER

And where I live,
I have fields at the back,
And at the front the Owendoher
River,
Now flowing slack.
But the river is an attraction
For birds,
And squawky coots, and moorhens,
Are heard.
And mallard can be seen as they
Swim upstream,
Or rest on the bank,
And their feathers preen.
The kingfisher is seen,
With his colours bright,
And the grey heron,
In graceful flight.

OH SEPTEMBER

Hail to you September,
Month of the hanging elder.
And evenings that chill,
But not enough to kill.
The trees in their green
Down,
Will soon turn brown.
And days still pleasantly
Warm,
But not so warm,
As to scorch, or harm,
And evenings of calm.

EARLY SEPTEMBER

As I sit here alone,
Strong winds, whip around
My home.
The trees bend,
In the wind,
Summer's end.
Early September upon us
Thrust,
With gale gusts.
And during the night,
A cold front,
Put to flight,
What was left of summer's
Heat,
As seasons meet.
A temperature fall,
Autumnal.

MID SEPTEMBER

Summer is over,
Autumn knocking on the door,
A year older,
In hedgerow, bramble,
And elder.
And rose hips,
As yet unripe,
Nature's fruits,
Of many types.
Days with the temperature,
Around plus ten,
Frost will soon,
Be back again.

LATE SEPTEMBER GALES

The late September gales,
That crossed,
And bent the trees, and tossed.
Huge waves lashed the coast,
No ships can cross,
No passengers, on or off.
Tory Island again cut off.

THROUGH THE SEASONS

AUTUMN POEMS

ℭ℞

BROWN AND GOLD

It was nice to behold,
The sun on the leaves,
Brown, and gold.
Only a pity that they will
Not hold.
But fall away through rain,
And cold.

FALLING LEAVES

Farewell the leaves your colour
Gold,
A few short months, and you
Are old,
And go away, as days get cold.
But in the spring, they will
Renew,
Another crop of leaves,
Like you.

LATE AUTUMN

Early November,
And of winter a hint,
The chimney smoke,
Is downward bent.
An East wind,
Cold on the face,
October now bows out,
With grace.
There are the last remaining
Elderberries,
The song thrush,
No longer merries.
Into silence he has lapsed,
Like the fallen leaves collapsed.
The trees now,
Are almost bare,
Winter now,
Is surely here.

A NIGHT SO BAD -THE ROAD TO ALLEN'S PUB[9]

I went in my hair all scattered,
Not that it mattered.
They looked at me, as if I was mad,
Why was I out,
On a night so bad?
The westerly gale,
Did prevail.
A darkened road,
With street lights none,
And the wind through the wires
Hum.
The road to Rockbrook,
A chore,
But better than television,
Bore.

---

[9] Allen's pub mentioned here, Is now known as the 'MERRY PLOUGHBOY.' It is just before you come to Rockbrook.

DECEMBER BLACKBIRD

Early December blackbird sings,
Thinking it is into spring.
I thought maybe he's a fool,
Around the corner weather cruel.
I felt for him, a little sorrow,
Who knows what will be tomorrow.

SEVEN MIGRATING LAPWINGS[10]

In a V shaped formation,
And flying low,
Westward from the coast they go.
They are wise, and no fools,
They are fleeing, the winter cruel.
They're safer by flying west,
Away from Europe's frozen wastes.
Where they came from, we can't be sure,
Far off Holland,
Or a frozen moor.
Who knows where,
They will be found,
Somewhere on unfrozen ground.
In the midlands,
They may take their rest,
Or in far off Mayo,
In the west.

[10] Seen over Dublin November the 9th.
In the 1980's.

THE MOON ON THE SNOW

The full moon, on the snow,
White,
Gave off great light.
The snow an off white hue[11],
A hint of blue.
A bright night.

---

[11] a word meaning colour. Written in February 2009 after a heavy fall of snow in Dublin.

A SUNDAY EVENING IN FEBRUARY

A Sunday evening damp, and quiet,
It's a gift,
You can't buy it.
The cars go by, but only few,
And not long ago, the cock,
He crew.
The great tit, in the distance,
Scolds,
He's staking out his territory
Bold.
Now near spring,
He'll soon have a brood,
I could hear his scold,
And it withstood.
There is little noise, or din,
It holds it's own peace within.

WINTER'S GRIP

Winter now tightens it's grip,
And the sun to bed, early slips.
While the sun shines,
It has no power,
And all that's left,
Are hardy flowers.
Fronts and gales,
Across the land whip,
And in between,
The temperature dips.

A RING AROUND THE MOON[12]

An early morning dark,
And a ring around the moon.
An old saying a remark:
    "It will be raining soon"

    It was right again,
It was pouring rain by ten.

---

[12] A ring around the moon is a sure Sign that rain is coming.

MILD SPELL – A FEBRUARY POEM

Mid February, and of spring a hint,
Maybe days from spring just lent,
The westerly gales have relent.

I would welcome it if it would
Stay.
But maybe in March,
We will pay,
With inclement weather,
Come our way.

I won't make any plans just yet,
For country walks,
And warm sunsets.
I'll be patient,
And my time I'll bide,
April, and May, be more relied.

THE PET PONY[13]

The pet pony,
And him only,
Was out the back,
In the vegetable plot,
The potatoes pulled,
But not the lot,
He was digging potatoes,
With his foot,
To eat them,
To tell the truth.
And I thought he was,
A dumb brute.

---

[13] This is a true story. This incident happened in Edmondstown in the early 1980's, when a pony was put into the field, after all the potatoes were pulled. But not all the Potatoes were pulled.

FAREWELL THE LEAVES OF AUTUMN

Farewell the leaves, of gold, and amber,
The year is now, a dying ember,
A scorching summer, we will remember.

Farewell the leaves, a colour golden,
A year well on, gone to olden.

Farewell the leaves, you look nice just,
Hanging there in gold, and rust.

Farewell the leaves, your fine display,
Of colour, before gone away.

Farewell the leaves, your purpose filled,
The summer is over,
And the evenings chilled.

Farewell the leaves, our path you soften,
We shuffle, as the evenings shorten.

Farewell the leaves, you bare the timber,
Goodbye October, hello November.

TWO BULLFINCHES

Two bullfinches graced my Sunday
Afternoon,
And fed on seeds,
On top of weeds,
My eyes were pleased.
And flew away so soon.

CR

CONCLUSION

SOME LATE POEMS AND SATIRES

❧

LITERATURE

I would contribute to literature,
If I could make words sound,
Like an overture.
If I could make them sound,
Just like the fiddle,
End to end,
No gaps, in the middle.
If I could make them sound just
Like the guitar,
Just as sweet as a bar.
And that is how it would be,
If only I could find the key.

TREASA

She told her story, [14]
In the paper "ALIVE", [15]
Of how she arrived.
Forsaking her house,
And her teaching career,
She arrived here,
At the Novitiate gate,
An act of faith.
After years of soul searching,
Inward reaching.
Her brother tragically killed,
A young death,
A test of faith.
Her brother knocked down by a car,
In the USA,
A country afar.
She rose above her crisis,
And now she wrote her thesis.
She said she would be embracing,
"Community, obedience,
Humility, spirituality"

---

[14] A young woman enters the convent - A true story.
[15] The paper ALIVE is a Catholic paper which comes out monthly.

a young woman,
she was raised in the Catholic
ethos,
the mass, the liturgy,
the cross.
Now she would be cut off,
From home, the family,
Humanity,
For her LORD,
As she said,
In her own words.
Embracing virtue,
And what is good,
Sisterhood.
Climbing the cold stairs,
In the
Order of SAINT CLARE'S,
A year of meditation and
Prayers.
We don't know how the story
Closes,
As she went into the order
Enclosed.

VILLANELLE[16]

I love Heaney's poem Villanelle,
Pray tell,
His best as well.

From the start,
A work of art.
A piece,
A masterpiece.

Carefully chiselled,
Like a sculpture,
Literature.
With careful interjections,
To perfection.

I've read a lot of poetry '
The rest.
It's among the best.

---

[16]Written October 2011, on Seamus Heaney's poem "Villanelle for an Anniversary" 1986.

AN AGONY AUNT - THE YOUNG BARMAID[17]

In the local pub, cum restaurant,
I have become, an agony aunt.
The young woman, barmaid,
And blonde,
Goes beyond.
She tells me her woes, everything,
And I can do nothing.

I just sit here,
A sympathetic ear.
She says she might emigrate,
Close the gate.
She hands me her soul,
On a plate.
She mentions New Zealand,
Canada,
New agenda.

---

[17] Written in 2013. This is a true story. This barmaid works in the Castle Inn in Rathfarnham Village. However, she did not emigrate from Ireland.

It would be unwise,
For me to advise.

I can only grieve,
I know she doesn't,
Want to leave.
She sees no future,
Now or soon,
In Ireland's economic ruin.
She talks economics,
Avoiding politics,
And me platonic.

Her part time bar work,
Pint glasses filled,
Earning little money,
Her life unfulfilled.

THE CELTIC TIGER WAS BAD
BUT... AN AFTERTHOUGHT[18]

The Celtic Tiger was bad but,
For all of that,
We had the building sites,
the hard hats.
we had employment,
we had enjoyment
but it had it's downside,
workers were downsized
We brought in immigrants,
immigration,
to subject them,
to exploitation.
But what we have now is worse,
An economic collapse,
An emigration curse.
We are exporting our youth,
To far off lands,
Canada, Australia,
New Zealand.
Can we ever get Ireland
Back on track,
Off the rack,
To be,
A country that attracts.

---

[18] Written in 2013.

THE BARMAN IN THE CASTLE INN (RATHFARNHAM VILLAGE) [19]

He is a barman, in the Castle Inn,
He is from Greece,
He is fit, and thin.
He is agile,
He gives you a dry smile.

He plays his cards,
Close to his chest,
He tells you a little,
Holds back the rest.
He works there some nights,
He gives you soundbites.

One night to the amusement,
Of the staff and me,
He broke into a little dance,
A fling.
Is this a Greek thing?

---

[19] A true story – written in December 2012.

Sometimes you don't know,
What he is saying,
When he speaks.
It's all Greek.

They say that he flies,
Back and forward,
Between Ireland,
And Greece,
A release.

Everyone makes him feel,
At home,
Now he's in a poem.

THE YOUNG CHINESE WOMAN
BLENDING IN.

It was funny to see,
The young Chinese woman,
The fan.
She was wearing her blue [20]
Supporter's tee shirt,
On O'Connell bridge,
Abridged.
Supporting Dublin,
To win.

She was of Oriental race,
And kin,
She was supporting Dublin,
To win,
She was blending in.

---

[20] This is a true story. During the summer, and the GAA, championship, supporters wear blue shirts, for their matches). Written in 2013.

A HIGHER JUDGEMENT[21]

I would prefer,
A higher judgement
God knows, what I meant.

Than the judgements,
Of man,
They don't know my plan.

They don't know,
My intent.
I would prefer,
A higher judgement.

---

[21] Written in 2013.

IRELAND'S BUDGET 2012 -[22]
BERLIN, AND THE GESTAPO - THE
REICH.

Ireland's budget 2012,
Was given the green light, to go.
It was sanctioned in Berlin,
By the Gestapo.

We have Merkel's face,
On the white part,
Of the Irish flag,
Flying over the GPO,
Also sanctioned by,
The Gestapo.
Ireland is in step,
Goosestep.

It's like, another Reich,
With tax hikes.
We will all be poor,
We will have to sell our cars,
We'll be back on bikes.

---

[22] Satire – December 2012.

THE ELECTION TRAIL 2011 - A POISONED CHALICE

Cynical satire.

The politicians, were seen,
    On the election trail,
    Giving details.
    Drink from our poisoned chalice,
    No drink from OUR poisoned chalice.
    They make up a stew,
    A witch's brew.

    Into the pot go all the details,
    Rats, and frogs, and puppy dogs tails.

    We eat it up, you and I,
    We die.

    The politicians, offer gravies,
    Shaking hands, with grannies,
    Kissing babies.
    And a new development,
    It has to be said,
    Patting dogs, on the head.[23]
    HEAVEN HELP US.

---

[23] A politician was seen during the election campaign, patting a dog on the Head. Will dogs get a vote?

IRELAND'S ECONOMY AND STATUS[24]

We are wooing the Chinese,
If you please,
Irish milk, and cheese.
Ireland for sale,
At a price,
A bag of rice.

Our economy is in the bin,
We are not a Banana Republic,
We are a banana skin.

All aboard the EU Mystery Train,
Tickets sold,
By IMF, EU, and Troika,
All off to NARNIA.

---

[24] Dark satire – February 2012.

NEW YORKERY, SHAMROCKERY, AND PADDYWHACKERY - SAINT PATRICK'S DAY[25]

It's all New Yorkery,
Shamrockery,
And Paddywhackery.

The politicians won't be seen,
They'll be in New York,
Wearing green.

Ireland is up to its neck in debt,
We'll drink green beer and we'll
Forget.

After all it is Saint Patrick's Day,
The whole world will go green,
For a day,
Even in Beijing far away.
We'll forget our troubles,
For a day,
Because that is the Irish way.

---

[25] A cynical satire – March 2012.

FAITH[26]

If you have faith,
Simple, and plain,
It will take you,
To a higher plane.

Now you believe,
Your secular world,
You will leave.

Now you have commitment,
Now you have contentment.

You may pay a price,
For your sacrifice.

You may become,
A lamb to the slaughter,
Criticised,
At every quarter.

---

[26] "Taking the shield of faith" - Saint Paul's epistle to the Ephesians'.
Written in 2013.

PRESERVED[27]

I do not claim,
To be a prophet,
I do not write,
Just for profit.

Some of my poetry,
Is sublime,
I hope it lasts,
The test of time.

It is easily understood,
A force for good?

I hope that it will,
Be preserved,
I have given my time,
I have served.

---

[27] Written in 2013.

EGOIST[28]

I will write what I can,
I insist,
But tell me,
If I am becoming,
An egoist.
That was not my agenda,
My list.

I am writing,
The poetry, and fiction,
That I missed,
I have a list,
But I don't want to become,
An egoist.

---

[28] Written in 2013.

IRELAND IN CHAINS – IRELAND'S WOES

What will be left,
For posterity?
Austerity?
The Celtic Tiger,
Ended in tears,
A society that is,
Two tiers,
Rich man,
Poor man,
No coherent plan.

A country wounded,
And marked,
Social justice,
Moved, and parked.
An accumulation,
Of debt,
Bloodlet.
Can we ever get,
A society, just,
And fair?
A profit margin,
A wage that's fair.

Ireland in hock,
Dry dock.
Ireland in chains,
Debts remain.
Ghost estates,[29]
Factories closed,
Locked gates.
We must get Ireland,
Up and running,
A second coming.
Not for our sakes,
But for the next,
Generation's sake.

---

[29] Ghost estates were housing estates, built by builders, during the boom years. Some of the builders ran out of money, and the estates remained unfinished. These estates became known as Ghost estates. Written in 2013.

IS DUBLIN CITY CENTRE DYING?[30]

Is Dublin City centre dying
No lying.
Less footfall,
Is the writing on the wall?

Shops paying,
Higher rent,
Less money spent.
How is it fair?
Higher bus fares?

No parking kerbs,
Motorists driven out,
To the suburbs.
Don't park here,
Don't park there,
Don't turn left,
Don't turn right,
Restrictions,
Everywhere.

---

[30] Written in 2013.

With less income,
Less people come.
A few tourists,
In the pubs,
Pub grub.
A few tourists,
At corners stand,
Maps in hand.
But less footfall,
Overall.
Will the shutters,
Come down?
Will Dublin become,
A ghost town?

THE HUMBLE BUMBLEBEE[31]

In my gardening magazine,
I see,
a write up on the bumblebee.
And what has that got to do
With gardening
Indeed,
We read.
The humble
Bumble,
Works for hours,
Pollinating, our fruit bushes,
And flowers.
And we are told,
He can tolerate,
Reasonable cold.
The bumblebee,
Works for free,
Unaware of you, and me.

POETRY[32]

Poetry,
Should bring new thoughts,
Brought,
Afterthoughts.

Poetry,
Should shed new light,
On what is wrong,
And what is right.

Poetry,
Should say things plain,
Take us,
To a higher plane.
With no sophistication,
Within,
Just do what it says,
On the tin.

---

[32] Written in 2013.

EMIGRATION[33]

They are in the Airport
Terminals,
Is Ireland's crisis,
Terminal?

Our youth,
Are departing,
Sad partings.

There is no work here.
Can Ireland's economy ever
Move up a gear?

They are Ireland's new
Export,
Baggage, suitcase,
Passport.

---

[33] Written in 2013.

I TRUST IN GOD - THE BIGGER PICTURE[34]

I trust in God,
For the bigger picture,
The crucifixion,
The resurrection,
A fixture.

Christ died,
To atone,
And to make room,
He was in the tomb,
He rolled back,
The stone.

It is all part,
Of a bigger plan,
For man.
For longevity,
For humanity,
For eternity.

---

[34] Written in 2013.

CAN TWO EXPERTS AGREE ON ANYTHING?

Can any two experts agree?
One says we need austerity.
Another says:
Spend money, lets party.

Maybe the answer lies
In the middle,
Solve the riddle.
We may all end up,
With a fiddle.
Begging on O'Connell Bridge,
Abridged.
Begging for money,
That won't be funny.

How many souls,
Can you fit on O'Connell Bridge?
Abridged?

Bugger,
We'll all be beggared.

It beggars belief,
Too much austerity,
And we'll come to grief.

Ireland will shut down,
1913 lock out,[35]
2013 LOCKDOWN.

---

[35] During the all out strike in Dublin, in 1913, workers were locked out, and their just grievances weren't listened to. It was known afterwards as "The 1913 Lock out". Written in 2013.

FINAL OUTCOME[36]

It was all unplanned,
My poetry is gone,
To a foreign land.

My poetry is gone,
Overseas,
To Colleges,
And Libraries,
To be read by students,
At their ease.

My poetry is gone
Overseas,
Perhaps to leave,
A legacy,
Of poetry.

It is the final
Outcome,
All unplanned,
An artist,
Gets no praise,
In his own land.

---

[36] Written in 2013.

CRECHE (THE PUB)[37]

It was Sunday evening
Enmeshed,
The pub was like,
A crèche.
Tiny tots,
Running about,
Shouts,
Conversation
Drowned out.
Television on,
GAA match on,
A tiny tot,
With drawing,
And crayon.
A notice on the wall,
'children strictly,
Under control.'
But it wasn't that bad
Besides,
There is a social side.

---

[37] Written in 2013.

EPITAPH[38]

What shall they write,
On my epitaph,
On my behalf.

A poet reviled,
Who endlessly toiled.
A poet blamed,
Defamed.

A poet outed,
Routed,
His sincerity doubted.

A poet slabbed,
Backstabbed.

A poet pained,
Nothing gained,
On the sidelines,
Remained.

A poet berated,
Deflated,
Outdated.

A poet who moaned,
Tombstoned.

---

[38] Satire written in 2012.

A poet despised,
Ostracised.

A poet burned,
Spurned,
Scripts returned.

A whinger,
A cringer,
Drink binger.

A poet lampooned,
Fooled,
Barstooled.

His books assigned,
To dusty libraries,
To be read by bookworms,
At their ease.

IN MEMORY OF SEAMUS HEANEY[39]

For sure,
He was dedicated to
Literature.
Seamus worked hard,
From London to
Harvard.
Never envious,
Competing, or
Backbiting,
Just writing.
Seamus became an icon,
Without hurting anyone.
Famous on his own merit,
Writer, and poet.

His poems moving, from the
Farmyard,
To Harvard.
Spanning five decades,
Farmyard tools, and
Spades.
Pitchfork,
In his earlier work.
And he interspersed those,
With works of prose.

---

[39] Seamus Heaney RIP who died in August 2013. May he rest in peace.

Later, a turn around,
Running in the London
Underground.
Seamus's later poems,
On harder ground.
His best poems found,
In the book
"Opened Ground"

THE FINAL ACT[40]

It's at the end,
The final act,
For what it's worth,
For what it lacked.

I'll go I'll leave
The stage,
Perhaps as a fool,
Perhaps as a sage.
Let the reader decide,
Let the reader engage.

The end of the issues,
The end of the facts.
The curtain falls,
The final act.
